Hope you have a
"Peep"-tastic Day!! :)

~ Lisa Ayotte

To God, who makes ALL things possible!

"For it is in giving, that we receive." – Francis of Assisi

Punnypeeps.com
Bristol, CT 06010
www.lisa@punnypeeps.com
Logo Design by Joe Philippon @ www.joephil.com
Photographs copyright ©by Lisa Ayotte, Punny Peeps
Ordering Information: Special discounts are available on quantity purchases by corporations, associa-
tions, and others. For details, contact the publisher at the address above.
"Punny Peeps' Amusing Animal Jokes"— First Edition©2020
ISBN 978-1-95127-810-6
Printed in the United States of America

PUNNY PEEPS'
AMUSING ANIMAL JOKES

LISA AYOTTE

PEEP 1: What do you call a moose that plays instruments?

PEEP 2: *A moos-ician!*

PEEP 1: Why did the chickens cross the road?

PEEP 2: To get some *eggs-ercise!*

PEEP 1: Why did the wolf cross the road?

PEEP 2: Because he was *chasing* the *chickens!*

PEEP 1: What do you get when you mix crabs with apples?

PEEP 2: A *crab-apple* pie!

PEEP 1: Which kind of ant is the biggest?

PEEP 2: The *eleph-ANT!*

PEEP 1: What is gray, has four legs and a trunk?

PEEP 2: A mouse going on *vacation!*

PEEP 1: Where do fish get their hair cut?

PEEP 2: At the *bobber-shop!*

PEEP 1: What do you call a cow that does magic tricks?

PEEP 2: *Mooo-dini!*

PEEP 1: Why is a snail the strongest animal?

PEEP 2: Because it carries its *house* on its *back!*

PEEP 1: How does a pig get to the hospital?

PEEP 2: It goes in a *Ham-bulance!*

PEEP 1: What do you call a dog that has a fever?

PEEP 2: A *hot dog!*

PEEP 1: What did the lion say to his cub on her birthday?

PEEP 2: It's *roar* birthday!

PEEP 1: Why do zebras love to watch really old movies?

PEEP 2: Because they are in *black and white!*

PEEP 1: What do you call a cat that loves lemons?

PEEP 2: A *sour puss!*

PEEP 1: What kind of bird works at a construction site?

PEEP 2: A crane!

PEEP 1: What do you call a deer that costs one dollar?

PEEP 2: A *buck!*

PEEP 1: Why do alligators really like St. Patrick's Day?

PEEP 2: Because they're already *wearing green!*

PEEP 1: How did the tree feel after it met the beaver?

PEEP 2: *Gnawed* so good!

PEEP 1: What do you call polar bears in the jungle?

PEEP 2: *LOST!*

PEEP 1: Why did the bunny go to the hospital?

PEEP 2: Because it needed a *hop-eration!*

PEEP 1: What do sharks and computers have in common?

PEEP 2: They both have *mega-bites!*

PEEP 1: What is a dog's favorite instrument?

PEEP 2: A *trom-bone!*

PEEP 1: What is a puppy's favorite kind of pizza?

PEEP 2: *Pup-peroni!*

PEEP 1: What do you call pigs that play basketball?

PEEP 2: Ball *hogs!*

PEEP 1: How can a car be like a frog?

PEEP 2: When it is being *toad!*

PEEP 1: Why did the monkey like to play mini golf?

PEEP 2: Because he liked to practice his *swing!*

PEEP 1: Where do cows stay when they go on vacation?

PEEP 2: At a *moo-tel!*

PEEP 1: What do horses like to eat before dinner?

PEEP 2: *Horse d'oeuvres!*

PEEP 1: What did the cats say when they saw the sandbox?

PEEP 2: "That's a nice *bathroom!*"

PEEP 1: What do bees wear when it rains?

PEEP 2: Their *yellow jackets!*

PEEP 1: What kind of fish only swims at night?

PEEP 2: *Starfish!*

PEEP 1: What do you call a rabbit with lots of money?

PEEP 2: A *million-hare!*

We hope you had LOTS of fun, but now Punny Peeps have to run! We're off to make *some more* punny jokes. Being silly is the best and we know you must have your own favorite jokes that you love to tell. So...write them down and create your own characters and scenes that go along with them. Assemble it all together and you'll have your very own joke book!

Make sure to continue to spend LOTS of time reading & laughing every single day! And always remember...it's the "little" things that matter most. YOU can change the world-Be a good role model to all your own "peeps" today by being kind, spreading joy and loving one another! ☺

Punnypeeps.com